THE BEGINNING
OF A STORY

and

THE CONTINUATION
OF A STORY

By

Amy Wilson Carmichael

TABLE OF CONTENTS

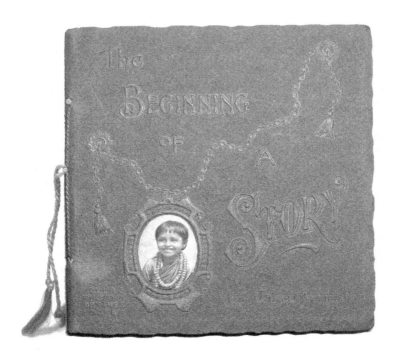

The Beginning of a Story

(To the Temple Children's Friends)

BY

AMY WILSON-CARMICHAEL

Keswick Missionary C.E.Z.M.S.

AUTHOR OF
"THINGS AS THEY ARE: MISSION WORK IN SOUTHERN INDIA."
"OVERWEIGHTS OF JOY," "LOTUS BUDS," ETC.

SECOND EDITION

MORGAN AND SCOTT LTD.
OFFICE OF *THE CHRISTIAN*
12 PATERNOSTER BUILDINGS
LONDON

NOTE. – This booklet only deals with South India. In both the Bombay and Bengal Presidencies, work (though on somewhat different lines) on behalf of children exposed to similar peril has been going on for years. So far as is at present known, the Temple child proper does not exist in all parts of India, as she does in the South; but even where the system has not been elaborated and consecrated by connection with the Temples, there is need for service on behalf of children in danger.

FRIENDS OF THE CHILDREN.--Miss Cavendish, Emsworth, Addlestone, Surrey, has formed a Guild of Prayer for the Temple children; any who wish to join it are asked to write to her.

Letters of enquiry about the garments worn by the children can be sent to Mrs. Billows, 33, Dornton Road, South Croydon; Miss A. Wilson, The Nook, Lathorn Villas, Folkestone; Mrs. Stewart, Levenwick, Levenhall, Musselburgh, N.B. Mrs. Stewart will also give information concerning the box which is sent to us each year.

For Australia, Mrs. Walter, Fern Hill, Kew, Melbourne, will give further news about the work.

Those who care to hear more will _find the story of our first Temple child told in full in "THINGS As THEY ARE "; "OVERWEIGHTS OF JOY" and "LOTUS BUDS" continue the tale.

FIRST EDITION . . . . . May . . . . . . 1908 . 5000 copies.
SECOND EDITION . . November 1910 . 5000 "

CHAPTER I. — THE BEGINNING

THE STORY OF the beginning of the work among Temple children is very simple. On March 6, 1901, our first Temple child was given to us. Before that, we knew there were Temple children, for we often saw them playing about the Temple women's houses. But we knew nothing more. After our first little girl became at home with us, she told us much about Temple life, and the desire to reach these little ones grew strong in us. We inquired among Christians and Hindus as to the best way to do something for them, but we were always told nothing had been done, or could be done, as the Temple women (sometimes the children's own mothers, oftener their adopted mothers) valued them far too highly to part with them. We found this true. Several times in our itinerating work we came across such children, and tried hard to save them, but always in vain.

In the autumn of 1903, when my comrades, Mr. and Mrs. Walker, had to go to England, I was much alone with the Lord Jesus. It was then that the burden of the little Temple children pressed so heavily that I could not bear it any longer — "Lord, what wilt Thou have me to do?" I asked, and the answer came quite clearly: "*Search for the little lost lambs with Me.*" And so the work began.

At first the difficulties seemed insurmountable. Few were interested in Temple children: still fewer thought it possible to save them. No one knew how to set about it. The first encouragement was the quickened interest shown by one of our evangelists, who had been itinerating in North Tinnevelly. When he returned, and I told him what the Lord

Jesus had said to me, he looked very much surprised. He told me how during his tour in the north for the first time in his life he had seen Temple women and children out in the streets at night; how it had stirred his heart; and how he and the pastor who was travelling with him had felt the shame of it, and the sin. "The sight penetrated us; it pierced us," he said. By comparing dates I found that the week of my waiting upon God was the week when the pastor and evangelist saw the sorrowful sight. I had asked Him to lay the burden upon our Indian fellow-workers, without whom we could not hope to do much; and He had done it. The evangelist wrote at once to the pastor, whose letter by return of post told us of a baby who was taken to a Temple woman when she was only four hours old. He set to work to save that little one, and soon had the joy of sending her to us — our first Temple baby.

As we went further into the work we found that the traffic in children is extensive. Little ones have been sent to us for safety from places hundreds of miles away. Constantly we have tidings of children in danger in still more distant districts. All over the Tami country we have found people on the watch for these children, and our difficulty has been to find them out before such watchers do. Once a child is adopted by a Temple woman or by one who intends to pass her on to a Temple woman, or use her in any other wrong way, that child is all but certainly quite out of reach. So our object must be to get hold of her before others have had the chance.

Children available for Temple Service (which means dedication to sin in the name of religion) usually belong to one of five distinct groups.

(1) Children are dedicated to the Temple because of a vow. For instance, the father is ill, and the mother vows that if he recovers she will give one of her children to the god. He recovers, and the child is given. (2) Sometimes the gift is

hereditary. A certain child in a certain family all down the generations is regarded as belonging to the god. (3) Sometimes a child is given in order to escape from some entanglement. A man marries out of caste and is outcasted; he soon tires of the inconvenience, gets rid of his wife, dedicates his child, is re-incasted and marries again. (4) Or a poor widow or a deserted wife of good family is faced by the impossibility of marrying her child suitably, so she "marries her to the god." (5) Finally, there is the unrecognised little babe, who, if of good caste and "fair to look upon," is considered well worth adoption. Whenever a little child is without its proper protectors, especially if the child is attractive, or shows promise of being afterwards attractive, you have a child in danger. All over South India there are men and women on the watch for such children. The gift or sale of a child for such a purpose is illegal; but money is not passed in public, and the necessary proof is unobtainable. The woman who buys the child calls her her own daughter, and can easily get witnesses to prove the relationship. But even if she could not, it would not matter, as the High Court allows adoption in the case of a Temple woman, although it is well known that such adoption invariably results in the child's being trained "to continue the succession."[1]

We believe our Government will eventually move; in the mean-time the children are perishing, and there is much to do. It is true that until pressure is brought to bear upon those responsible (the priests and the Temple women), pressure either from outside or from inside, the trade in little children will go on. Pressure from outside, caused by an amended *and carefully enforced* law, could hardly become speedily operative. Pressure from inside, caused by a quickened national conscience, seems distant. The reform movement moves very slowly. But it cannot be that this

---

[1] For further information upon this subject see "LOTUS BUDS."

whole generation of Temple children must pass unreached. There are twelve thousand Temple women in South India. Most of these women have adopted at least one child; many have adopted two. A child over eight or nine who has been much under Temple influence is usually too old in Temple life to be counted a little child at all. She cannot be put among ordinary children, unless she is exceptionally simple-minded. So that the next ten years must see a whole generation of little Temple children pass into Temple girls (and that means, humanly speaking, passing out of reach in a very real and awful way), unless within the next ten years we reach them while they are children — innocent little babies and innocent little girls.

What has been done towards reaching them is not much yet, but when we look back to the time when even less was done, we thank God and take courage. Three years ago we knew only two missionaries who had saved Temple children, or babies destined for the Temple. Each of the two had saved one such little child. We wrote to them asking for advice as to the best way to save more. Their letters were inspiring, because of the sympathy in them; but they felt as perplexed as we did when faced with the problem of how best to reach numbers. Now, from twenty-nine widely separated districts little ones have been sent to the Dohnavur nurseries. And in seventeen or more different centres Indian Christians and missionaries are on the watch for these children, and are seeking for them definitely. In some of the more distant centres new nurseries will be opened we trust in the near future, and thus new radiations will result.

But perhaps the greatest visible gain is the enlargement of knowledge the past three years have brought, and with it naturally has come a quickened conscience upon the subject. There was a time when even experienced missionaries doubted the very existence of these children; now no one doubts. Then, intelligent sympathy was rare; each letter which brought the inspiration of such sympathy is remembered gratefully; now, wherever we go we find kind hearts stirred to care. India is a vast land. As the note to this booklet says, we purposely confine ourselves to the South, and avoid all generalisations. With this proviso, I think it is true to say, that almost everywhere a new sympathy is springing up, a new keenness.

This, which so greatly helps our work, is not found alone among missionaries, without whose co-operation it would have been impossible to do what has been done, but among civilians (representatives of Government here) we have met with every possible kindness. Perhaps there is something in the helplessness of a little child which appeals to the Englishman; whatever the cause, the fact is pleasant to tell, we have never once met with anything but kindness from those in authority, though their power to help is limited.

Sometimes even orthodox Hindus help us. Their power is practically unlimited. A little girl of four (the Leela of the picture on the cover) was brought to us partly through the efforts of an orthodox Hindu, who realised the iniquity of dedicating such a little one to Temple service.

Sometimes we are able to pierce through to the heart of the system, and touch the Temple woman herself. One, after a long talk with our worker, admitted the wrong she had done in dedicating her first little daughter to this iniquitous life, and after she had been persuaded to give up her second child, a bright baby girl, who was to have belonged to another Temple, she was heard to say that she would dedicate no more. But this case is not typical. As a rule we find the grown-up Temple woman is so spoiled by her long training that her conscience is not easily approached. It is hardly her fault. She did not choose the life. She was doomed to it from infancy, nothing else ever opened before her. She is the result of her environment, an environment for which she is not responsible.

There is need for all that can be done all over South India to save little children from being doomed to such a life. By far the most serious wrong is the spiritual and moral injury inflicted. But there is another though a less important aspect which sometimes forces itself upon us. When English children ask us what it means to be a Temple child, we tell them such little girls are taught to be naughty, and never to be good, and sometimes they are whipped for wanting to be good. And sometimes they are punished just for wanting their own mothers, and shut up till they have forgotten them. This is quite enough for the child who asks, and when one thinks of it, it is enough for anyone. Almost everything that need be said is wrapped up in it.

A few weeks ago a friend, who during the past year has become aware of what is going on in the city where she lives, read a letter concerning the matter before a body of missionaries. When she had finished, a missionary present quietly told how he himself had heard the cries of a child at night, coming from a house near his own. He put the matter into the hands of the police, but with no result. Such a cry has a sound in it like the sound that long ago cried unto God from the ground.

CHAPTER II. – THE CHILDREN

FAR AWAY FROM such sounds is the quiet little old-world village of Dohnavur. It is nothing to look at, a mere huddle of mud huts without a street worth calling a street in the whole place. But it is backed by the Western Ghauts. Climb the church tower and you see them, almost encircling the plain where the village lies, with great protecting arms. You gaze and gaze till the eye, satisfied with beauty, drops to the nearer foreground and rests on trees, their green tops interlacing, and among the greenness the red roofs of houses. These are the nurseries.

Perhaps no safer and no healthier place could have been found for our little children. No place on the plain is very healthy, the insanitary villages are all too near; but we have a big beautiful field where the air blows, if there is any air to blow, straight across the open country from a gap in the hills. We did not choose Dohnavur. We were living here, itinerating in the country round, an almost entirely Hindu tract, with many wholly Hindu towns and villages scattered about upon it, when the work for the little children grew up about us, and before we knew it we were a family. Then we realised our blessings. The children can go for rambles in the fields around, no one making them afraid. The people all about are friendly. Once when a raid was planned upon the bungalow, the Hindus refused to join. "No, we are friends with the bungalow. We will not play the traitor." And the object, the seizing of a little girl, fell through. Then too we have all possible help and sympathy from our Indian Pastor, and Indian friends, so that although Dohnavur is inaccessible and inconvenient in many ways, we are at peace, believing that we are meant to be here. Visitors notice the restful atmosphere of the little place. There is a sense of detachment from the noisy modern world. There is time to be quiet, and to think, as well as do.

The nurseries are extremely simple, and all our ways correspond. But the simple buildings and the simple life generally suit us all, and the children thrive and are happy.

The children: I feel inclined to move in large circles about them rather than directly touch them. After all, what we see in a child depends very largely upon what we bring to it.

Passing through the outer nursery, used as a night nursery at present, we look out upon a little courtyard, cool and green, with caladium and fern, from which, on the other side, the two day nurseries open. There is a sudden scuttling, and we see what looks like a scattering of young rabbits to their warren. The explanation is that the babies, big and little, were playing in the courtyard, and, catching sight of a stranger, have scampered off, or toddled off, according to their several powers of progression, to spread the news. Presently an adventurer runs up to reconnoitre. She finds you are not formidable, and announces the fact by signals to the others, two or three of whom now advance with welcoming faces and outstretched little hands. From this point on there is no difficulty. The secret of making friends with babies is to leave them to make the first advances. You have not broken the nursery code of manners by rushing up to any individual, and seizing her against her will, so the nursery accepts you; and as a visitor, if nice, is a thing to be desired, you are first captured, then, as if the babies felt themselves responsible for your entertainment, you are invited to be amused.

With two eloquent and affectionate small people on your knee, and another standing on the box upon which you are sitting, with her arms tightly clasped round your neck, it is not easy to pay due attention to the overtures of No. 1 upon whose introduction you have been admitted to this intimacy. She is bent upon your acceptance of some broken pieces of pottery, an old reel, an invalid doll, a ball with a hole in its side, and a much-indented tin. This last is to thump on the floor, or to hit with the used-up reel. The noise it makes is delightful.

But No. 1 (for whom our private name is Puck) has other entertainments in reserve. Some weeks ago a gentleman visitor was observed to wash his hands in invisible water and then twirl his moustache. Puck did not appear to be noticing anything, but it is not her way to tell you all her thoughts. In reality this fascinating habit was duly noted, and immediately appropriated. And now you become aware that you are being shown by a baby of two what grown-up people do. The moustache incident is followed by others in quick succession. You do not know whether to laugh or be shocked.

No. 1 is still performing in this graceless fashion when a raid from behind surprises you, and you turn to see half a dozen living creatures about to precipitate themselves upon you. This suggests total extinction. You rise hurriedly, and, perceiving two swings hanging invitingly empty, you dispose of six small persons and breathe freely.

"Amma, look!" A child with a perfect tangle of curls and the brightest of dancing brown eyes is calling to you excitedly, and pointing to your old friend No. 1, also curly headed and with eyes too innocent. You look, and, horrified, behold that youthful irrepressible apparently attempting immediate suicide upon the crossbar of the swing. So you hasten to the rescue, to be received with derisive shouts of laughter, as No. 2 throws back her head in imitation of No. 1

with a perfectly dreadful recklessness. The nursery is not the place for people with weak nerves.

The acrobat baby is the little daughter of a Temple woman five hundred miles away, and the sinner who so enjoyed your dismay was to have belonged to a Temple two days' journey distant. No. 1 came to us a sick but always cheerful infant. She is the nursery wonder — its scamp and its pickle. No. 2 was from the first very naughty, but very dear; she is a loyal-hearted little soul, and very loving; but life is going to be difficult for her. She takes it too often by the wrong handle.

Sitting composedly in the same swing is a demure little tot of about the same age but very different in disposition. She has had a suffering infancy, but there is no look of pain in the placid little face. This baby comes from a Temple town three days to the East, and the droll little four-year-old, who is swinging the trio, pushing the swing crookedly sometimes, to their intense disgust, comes from a place a thousand miles to the North.

Another four-year-old is pushing the second swing. She was being carried off to a Travancore Temple when our messenger overtook the party, and persuaded her captors to release her. She was nearly mad with misery when first we saw her, but now is such an exceedingly lively little person that repression is occasionally necessary. In the swing there is a child with big serious eyes, which give no hint of the mischief within. She was all but given to one of our largest and most famous Temples. Next to her is a quaint little thing, who was to have belonged to a small Temple four miles distant. This little mite has had an adventurous infancy. We never thought we should see her here, a happy, healthy two-year-old. Cuddling close beside her, her fat hands holding on tightly to the rope, is a baby whose strong point is devotion to her friends. You may tumble her up anyhow, and hold her in the most uncomfortable position; you may scold her, ignore her, treat her in any way you choose; so long as you do not hurt her feelings by putting her down, she is content.

Trotting unsteadily about, but very proud of her shaky performance, is a small comical little girl, with a mop of curls which she persists in tumbling over her eyes. She is so like a Skye that no one can resist calling her Puppy. To every question put to her she nods her head decidedly; but if you accost her otherwise than by question, she is nonplussed, and considers you a trying sort of person. Then there is a dear little shy girl bordering on three, who studies you out of the corners of her eyes when you are not observing her; and another of three, not at all shy; and still another, shy, but friendly when sure of your intentions. And there a little one-and-a-half, very lovable, who upon her return to the nursery after any short absence diligently trots around her smaller sisters and embraces them all. This little one, the nursery pet, is only just beginning to talk, but she understands everything, and manages to express her little thoughts in vivid pantomime.

Distant a long day's journey[2] from Dohnavur is our branch nursery at Neyoor, which was opened so that our younger and more delicate infants should be near medical help. Neyoor is the centre of the London Missionary Society's Medical Mission in South Travancore. We hope eventually to be able to be all together at Dohnavur; but till that good time comes we are most grateful for the splendid help given to us by our L.M.S. comrades.

Among the Neyoor babies are some from distant places, the Telugu country, Canarese country, Marathi country, North Travancore, and all parts of the Tamil country, which extends four or five hundred miles to the

---

[2] Since this booklet was written new Nurseries have been built at Dohnavur, and all the children are there now.

north. Several who arrived at Neyoor so puny and fragile that we had little hope for them, are now beautiful, fat, strong babies, ready to be passed on to the Dohnavur nursery. There is a joy only known to those who have toiled and prayed for these little ones, when the toil is rewarded, and the look of suffering passes from the little faces, and the happy look of healthy babyhood comes instead.

Our brave Ponnamal, known to some by her translated name, Golden, is in charge of the Neyoor nursery. She is God's golden gift to the work. Under her there are young nurses, girl converts, and some older women, most of whom were also converts. These girls and women belong to different castes. In India, such work is usually undertaken by women of a special class, and no money would induce those of a different position to do it. Love must be the inducement. Ponnamal has been greatly helped to raise the standard, and teach these girls and women that all work is both noble and ennobling if done in the name of the Lord Jesus. At first it was most difficult to get to the end of the caste feeling on the subject, but Ponnamal herself quietly did the things they did not care to do, helped by two women whose natural work it was. Now there is not one of the nurses who would refuse to do anything. Something of her spirit has entered into them.

From another point of view we find the work most useful and helpful in providing an outlet for the natural woman longing for scope and someone to love. These converts have to give up all that makes life dear to a woman. Their hearts are often very empty. Too often then they turn, in heart at least, back to the home they have left. The care of a little child and the discipline in practical unselfishness such work involves has a wonderfully soothing and bracing effect upon the character, and the empty heart is filled again.

But naturally there are difficulties in the training, and if it were not for Ponnamal our nurses would not be what they are.

Through all the difficulties incidental to such work, through severe strains, and in times of stress that test the stuff of which the soul is made, her faith and courage and utter love have never failed. We do thank God for Ponnamal.

We keep in touch with our Neyoor nursery by means of almost daily bulletins and frequent visits. My last visit left a happy impression upon my mind. I arrived in the early morning and lived through the day's life with the babies. The first performance was very amusing. All the infants were put out to air while their respective nurses were about their morning's work. Some were laid on mats, some were swung in hammocks hung from a Jack fruit tree in the garden. Some were in swings. They seemed to understand it was useless to demand attention just then, and were very patient and contented. But the moment the nurses reappeared, each little infant began to protest, and it was evident they considered being put out to air a tiresome proceeding, only to be put up with when nothing better was in prospect. It was pretty to see how fond each baby was of her own nurse, and the nurse's motherliness explained the confiding affection. One very engaging little child had a way of nestling up close to her nurse when a stranger appeared, and from that safe refuge she would gravely study the intruder, till, satisfied that all was well, she would suddenly beam and make advances. How well we remembered this baby's arrival. She was saved just in time; Temple women were after her, and half an hour later we should not have got her. We remember how she lay in our arms, a lovely little babe, soft and pink like a little half-opened rose-bud. And as she gazed up at us with that serious wondering look so common in the eyes of young babies, oh how we thanked God the little one was safe!

CHAPTER III. — THE RAVENS

ALL WHO ARE busy themselves will recognise the impossibility of extensive correspondence. If we wrote all the letters we are asked to write, "just to tell a little about the work," there would soon be no work about which to tell. And yet it is natural that those who care should wish to hear, and we hope this booklet, which is meant to serve as an open letter to our friends, will meet such wishes. In these last pages I propose answering the questions which sometimes reach us. "What is your greatest need?" write some, "and how are your needs supplied?"

Our greatest need now — and always — is earnest, fervent prayer. Readers of Bishop Moule's "Colossian Studies" will remember the passage which deals with the Apostle's description of his prayer: "Striving according to His active force which is acting within me in prayer." "It was a manner of a wrestle of the soul. Visible or not to human eyes, it was this to his Lord — a sustained, importunate, courageous conflict; a strife with all and anything which would withstand his praying, and with all and anything which would suggest to him that his Lord was not listening, and would not bless. . . . Prayer was never meant to be indolently easy, however simple and reliant it may be," concludes a later paragraph, "it is an infinitely important transaction between man and God. And therefore very often, when subjects and circumstances call for it, it has to be viewed as a work involving labour, persistency, conflict, if it would be prayer indeed."

Remembering this view of prayer, and how much such prayer may cost, we still say, "Pray for us."

Our needs are supplied as Elijah's were, the children would tell you if you asked them. God sends His ravens. We have no provision made for us except what we share with the birds and the flowers; but it has never failed us.

We do not tell when we are in need, unless definitely asked, and even then not always; for often the leading seems to be silent, except towards God, and we fear lest our little children should seem to crowd in among the many claims to help which must press so heavily upon the hearts of givers at home, and intercept anything which should be sent elsewhere. We rely upon the verses which assure us that our Father knows our needs, and we take it that with such a Father, to know is to supply.

Sometimes His Fatherly foreknowledge has been proved in such visible fashion that it would be strange if we could ever be afraid. Dohnavur is so remote from the great South Indian highways, that there are no passers-by to call unexpectedly just when we are at the end of our resources, and drop surprises upon us. Most of our ravens fly to us by way of the daily post. Again and again we have been low, and no one outside our household has known anything about it; but before the last moment, for in a country place stores have to be bought in advance, enough has come to carry us over the wave. We remember a time of threatened famine, when prices were suddenly rising, and £20 was needed to lay in a stock of paddy (unshelled rice). That week brought us a single gift of £20 from a friend in England, whose very name up to that time was unknown to us. So the paddy was poured out in a great heap on the ground, and measured, and we paid for it with light and happy hearts. Again we remember a day when a letter came telling us of a child in danger far away. Sufficient money to meet necessary expenses must be sent off that same afternoon, or she would be otherwise appropriated, and from that appropriation there would be no release. We had not enough money in hand to pay for the chief charge, the long journey of those who would bring her to us; and no money could possibly reach us, even if we sent a coolie with a cheque to cash, for two days from that time. While we were reading the letter, our good postman, who is a sort of visible Raven, came up joyfully with a roll of rupees in his hand. The older children, who are in our confidence, know the look and the meaning of such a roll of rupees, and there was a glad call of "Money order!" It was a money order from Canada, enough to cover all the expenses connected with that little child's deliverance. Usually gifts come to us by cheque, and there is always delay in getting a cheque cashed. That day our need was ready money, and here it was in our hands. We piled the silver on the floor, and knelt down round it and thanked God. It meant the redemption of the dear little Puck of the preceding chapter. Do you wonder we were glad? At such times we realise that whoever may be our Postmaster-General, or however the foreign post-office is conducted, the whole intricate system is under one supreme control.

But it would be untruthful to leave an impression of unvarying experiences such as these. We could tell many such to the glory of our Father, without whom never a sparrow falls to the ground, or a little human nestling; and it is tempting to linger over stories of gladness because each little incident has been such a cheer and joy. But sometimes things are otherwise.

We lately hung a picture of Elijah and the ravens in the babies' nursery. No. 1, the intelligent Puck, was immediately deeply interested, and the picture was explained to her. She studied it awhile. The prophet in brilliant blue is sitting on a rock in yellow sunset light, a streamlet yellow as the sky flows at his feet. Three faithful ravens bearing substantial provisions are close at hand, but one bird is apparently concerned in getting a drink of water for himself. He had probably already done his part, for a piece of very red meat lies on the rock beside Elijah; but this possibility was not recognised for the moment, and a disapproving finger was pointed to the supposed defaulter. "That crow," observed Puck, "has brought nothing at all."

Sometimes, mail day — the day we specially look for the coming of the ravens — passes without the arrival of anything convertible into bread and meat. The letters on my breakfast plate look promising, but as one after the other is opened, and nothing more than kind assurances of interest and requests for descriptive letters is found therein, we are reminded of the critical Puck, "That crow has brought nothing at all." But let no one, richer in faith than in this world's goods, misunderstand me. We do not count prayer "nothing at all." Letters which tell of prayer strengthen our hearts, and set us watching with all the more confidence for the coming of the ravens another day.

Naturally, our greatest need, next to prayer, is just the simple straightforward need of money — to feed our little ones and clothe them, and to provide for the long journeys connected with their redemption, and all other expenses bearing upon the salvation of Temple children. Nurseries (so necessary too) are never built except with money specially so marked by the givers. Few of our workers take anything beyond their bare expenses, so that most of what comes is free to be used directly in the redemption and care of the children. Cheques may be sent to the Lay Secretary, C.E.Z.M.S., Lonsdale Chambers, Chancery Lane, London, W.C., with a note naming their destination; or the gift may be sent to the Secretary and Manager, Bank of Madras, Madras, for the C.E.Z.M.S. Dohnavur account, upon receipt of which the Manager will advise me and credit it to the Mission account. Any bank will undertake this transaction, and save the giver all trouble. Or a draft, cheque, or postal order may be sent to me; or, most welcome of all, if the commission is not prohibitive, a money order may be sent to the Dohnavur Post Office, Tinnevelly. This reaches me in rupees; and, as the story of little Puck's deliverance shows, it is sometimes a very God-send to receive the gift in cash. By whatever way it is sent, it should be named as for the Nurseries, not as for any individual child.

When letters come asking what it costs to adopt a child, we answer that we have no children adopted upon a money basis. We are most grateful to anyone who will adopt a little one as a Prayer-child. We want all our children to have many Prayer-relations, just as when we were small we had many relations who loved us enough to pray for us. We send the name of a little child, or if it is preferred an older girl, or a worker, to anyone who will accept this great responsibility. We do not promise to write often to the Prayer-relations; but if at any time a post-card comes asking for news of the Prayer-child, we promise to reply at once by post-card if not by letter. When any special need arises, I send what we call a Prayer-telegram to the Prayer-relations, and often we have found this the quickest way to communicate with them. This Prayer-child plan has worked most happily. It satisfies the natural desire to have a child specially one's own. And the bond is all the stronger because it is forged, not of the gold that perisheth, but of that which endureth and will endure through all Eternity. The older children know the names of their Prayer-relations, and pray for them too. What delightful meetings and recountings there will be one day!

As to the actual cost of any individual child, we do not feel it possible to answer correctly; and even an estimate would be misleading at present. Our accounts are complicated by the fact that we are both hospital and nursery combined. We constantly need not only large quantities of fresh milk, but condensed milk, and milk foods and medical nutrients. These things cost considerably more by the time we have paid commission, carriage, and customs duty, than they do at home; and when this is remembered, anyone experienced in the care of little children, especially very delicate little children, will understand that nurseries are expensive delights. But they are repaying expenses. Looked at from the lowest point of view, no one who knows from what these little ones are saved could doubt that for a moment; and the pleasure of seeing the happy, healthy, little girls, and perfectly contented babies, where before all was fretfulness and weariness, is a pleasure that must compensate for much. We feel that nourishment is the last thing in which we dare economise, if our children are to grow up glad and strong and useful.

Later, when they can live mainly upon curry and rice, the food cost drops rapidly; but then comes another expense of almost equal importance. Some of our little ones show signs of a bright intelligence which should be cultivated. India needs leaders, medical women, nurse evangelists and teachers. Such workers require a special course of training. If this more liberal view commends itself to the Temple Children's friends, it will mean that in the future, if there is to be a future, something more generous than the least possible co-operation will be required. And so we earnestly say to all who care for our little children, ask Him who has so marvellously redeemed them what His purpose in their redemption is, and what share in that purpose He would have you take. Think, too, of the many not saved yet; and then, "Whatsoever He saith unto you, do it."

We have said that we have proved that the Prayer adoption plan works smoothly; we should have added that it has been a blessing to the children. We have often been able to trace improvement in a little child from the date when one or more Prayer-relations took up the burden of that little life. It would be strange if it were not so; and yet it is good to see that it is so. We have found, too, that the plan creates and maintains just that touch which is so uniting. Frequent letters are not required when we meet daily, perhaps oftener, in the place where distance is not measured. Many of those who have adopted Prayer-children send us what they can towards the Nursery, and doubtless the gift comes with many a loving thought for their own special little possession; but they know that the money is used for the need of the day. We have no supported and unsupported children; for they all share alike what their Father sends. We are very grateful to those who so trust us to use their gifts for the good of our children; and we seek to be guided in the spending so that the gifts may return to the givers in joy and blessing for ever.

Is the work worth doing? It is a question seldom asked now; but lest even one who reads should wonder over it, may I say to such a one, share with us a little of the gladness wrapped up within it; forget all the anxieties, the heart-breaks, the wearinesses — they fade to utter forget-fulness, blotted out by such a memory as last Palm Sunday brought us. It was the baptism of some of our older children, our first to confess Christ in baptism. They were standing in a semicircle on the sand by the water-side and round them a ring of converts, now workers, each with a little child in her arms; for the babies were with us that day so that their nurses could come. One by one the children walked into the water, and we on the shore were watching, when from the far West, over the mountains, a flood of glorious light streamed out upon us all, till the children in the water seemed bathed in liquid gold. It was so sudden and so glorious that instinctively we looked up, almost expecting to see something seen but once — long, long ago; and the glory of it flashed through us, laying bare for one brief moment all the inwardness of joy deep under reach of speech.

Do not such moments come to all who have known something of a walk "with Christ at midnight over moonless seas"? Moments when the joy is so exquisite that the heart knows well it is not of earth? It is just a note dropped from the song of the Lord our God and our Redeemer, just an overflow of that transcendent joy. But it is enough for us, enough till the mortal has put on immortality. More would be too much. And yet it is only one flash of the light of gladness that the moment must mean to Him.

And now, in sympathy still, share something different with us. It was an afternoon some months later. Two of us were visiting a Temple-house in a neighbouring town, when we saw standing in the doorway a little girl of seven or eight, with the unrelieved gloominess of an unlighted room behind her. The Temple woman in the courtyard explained her fragile appearance by saying she had been ill; and though the little girl had evidently been kindly tended, there was something so desolate and lonely in her attitude as she glanced at us with the uninterested listlessness of a tired child, that we who saw her have not been able to forget her ever since.

We had already tried to save that little one, but she had reached the age when she is of value to her adopted mother, and she smiles at the mere thought of parting with her. Nor would the child willingly come; the Temple house is home to her. But we show her to our questioner, and we say earnestly: Think! Think of the future opening there. Think of that little shrinking girl being led out to meet it till she shrinks back no longer. Think of all that is sweet and simple passing quite away, never, never to return. Think of the influence to be exercised by and by. Think of the scars those little hands will brand on hearts one day. Think of the dishonour to the holy name of God!

Out in another courtyard other children played— Temple children too, with a fate as dark in store; and their play held its appeal, as something very innocent seen amid sinful surroundings ever must, but for us that evening the little girl in the doorway with the background of darkness behind her was the unconscious type.

Two hours later we were back in the nursery. Loving, noisy, crowding little people were round us in a moment, all wanting to climb into our arms at once, all wanting to be kissed at once. We might have been away from them for a week, they were so welcoming. But among all the dear little faces we could not help seeing one so different; the little form with its air of solitariness seemed to have come in with us; among all the merry children seemed to stand in her unchildlike silence and unapproachable aloofness that little Temple child.

Is it worth while saving such, while still they can be saved? O friends to whom we write, need we answer the question?

We should be most grateful for prayer that as the work grows larger it may grow in depth and in earnestness of purpose. Also we would ask prayer for the young convert-girls now growing up, that they may be kept safe and fitted to be a blessing to others.

END

MORGAN & SCOTT LTD., office of The Christian, 12 Paternoster Buildings, London.

The Continuation Of A Story

BY

AMY WILSON-CARMICHAEL

Keswick Missionary C.E.Z.M.S.

AUTHOR OF
"THINGS AS THEY ARE: MISSION WORK IN SOUTHERN INDIA."
"OVERWEIGHTS OF JOY," "LOTUS BUDS," ETC.

RING A RING OF ROSES

A JOY-SONG

For the quiet joy of Duty,
Praise, praise I sing,
  For the commonplace and lowly,
  But with pleasure high and holy
  In each unromantic thing,
  Praise, praise to Thee, my King.

For the solemn joy of Battle,
Praise, praise I sing,
  For the wounds and sore distresses,
  For the love which soothes and blesses,
  Strength in weakness perfecting,
  Praise, praise to Thee, my King.

For the splendid joy of Triumph,
Praise, praise I sing,
  For the joy all joys excelling,
  Passing, passing human telling,
  Joy to see Thee conquering,
  Praise, praise to Thee, my King.

FOREWORD

IS THE "Beginning of a Story" never going to have a Continuation? This is the question which comes rather frequently and seems to expect an answer. The answer is that we are in the middle of the Continuation, and it is difficult to stop and talk about it, for continuations, if they are to continue, insist upon steady work rather than over-much talk. I am reading Florence Nightingale's Life just now, and this sentence exactly expresses my feeling as regards writing: "She cared for writing only as a means to action." However, perhaps a booklet might be a means to action. With this hope "The Continuation" goes out to do its work.

CHAPTER I.

TEN YEARS AGO we began the Nursery work in a little, long, low mud-room, which was kitchen, food-room, night and day nursery, all in one. Now we have spread into nine nurseries and a kindergarten (overcrowded at the moment of writing), and are in the throes of building several new cottage nurseries. Crawling round the compound is a wall which, when finished, will be nearly a mile long. Truly we are in the middle of the Continuation.

But to my mind the evidences to this happy fact are even more discernible outside the compound than in it Ten years ago to mention the Temple children was to court an incredulous smile or that peculiar sort of silence which chills the very marrow in one's bones. "No such children in this city," wrote a missionary of forty years' experience to Mr. Walker, when, in order to collect facts for me, he wrote to certain of his brethren. He also wrote to Indian brethren, known to himself as men who had pierced under the surface of things as few, even Indians, have; and from that city came tidings of secret marriages of young children to the gods; and to that city we traced not tens but scores of little ones, only four of whom we were ever able to reach. "Have you seen the myth?" asked another missionary of one who had been staying with us at Dohnavur. To him as to many another. Temple children were creations of an imagination more ardent than informed.

There were, as I have told before, some who knew the truth. The first two to encourage me by believing in the need to do some- thing can never be forgotten in the Story of

Beginnings. They were Canon Margoschis of the S.P.G. and Mrs. Hayson of the American Madura Mission. These two friends wrote letters that were precious to me, for they too had burned over the wrong done to the children. But even they could find no way to help. They had saved one or two such children, but they could not suggest any way by which others could be reached; they could only cheer one on in what seemed a forlorn hope. But praise God for forlorn hopes, for impossibilities, for blank walls rising straight up overhead. Such things are challenges.

And there were others, blessed be every one of them, who backed up the new enterprise from the beginning, whose eyes once opened could not be closed again. Gradually the number grew till now there are few great districts in South India and few countries in the world where we have not friends upon whom we can count for all that friends can give; from the first there were men in the I.C.S. who knew the truth, and who cared, cared intensely some of them; for the wrong to those innocent children touched all the manhood in them. The sympathy, and where it was possible, co-operation, of such has always been a strength.

But there are still among us the incredulous and indifferent. We are only continuing to learn ourselves and to enlighten others; we have not finished yet. As if by way of strange proof to the truth of this, an A B C book, lately published in an Eastern city and dedicated to a little child, has been given to me. The taste of several of the pictures is questionable, but there can be no question where the drawing intended to illustrate the letter N is concerned. One can only believe that the woman whose work this book is, is ignorant of what the word "Nautch" means, and it is this ignorance which accounts for the heartless treatment of the subject. "She shall have music wherever she goes," says the jingle appended to the drawing. Yes, but what music? Verily, there is need to continue to tell those who will listen what these things mean.

Once, invited by a friend who knew something of the truth touching these matters, I met a group of men each notable in his way. Most belonged to the legal world, one to an Indian Court, one to an Indian Society for the betterment of India. The matter under discussion was the framing of a law to protect children from wrong. Two of the ten men were in earnest, the other eight enjoyed the talk preparatory and attendant upon all action in India, but they saw no tremendous reason for immediate exertion of any sort. The evil was decreasing: education, civilization, these elevating influences would gradually and pleasantly permeate society. In the meantime, we asked, what about the perishing children? Ah, it was sad, doubtless; that they should perish was indeed regrettable. But after all were there many imperilled? For his part one old gentleman doubted it, though doubtless, he added cheerfully, unaware of the force of his admission, "a change in the law is much required."

Yes, it is much required; but let it be remembered that good though (we trust) the now nearly approaching change will be, it will not end the evil, it will not end the need for the work we are doing. No blessed full stop to this work is in view yet, nor can it be till India itself in its inward parts is renewed and purified.

CHAPTER II.

LIFE IS A curious thing, it deals in so many and such various points of view. The mere talker, the surface-skimmer, airily dismisses the unpleasant. We, down in the dust of just that very thing, do not find it so easy to dismiss. Here are two or three stories from the last year's sheaf, for, "decreasing" or not, the thing with which we have to deal continues.

A fortnight ago a post-card, scribbled all over with fine Tamil writing, told of a child in danger in a town a day's journey distant from Dohnavur. "Send at once, bringing only a seeley" (Tamil dress), concluded the post-card, and wondering what would arrive, we sent.

Two days later a little girl of about eight, clad in our blue seeley, stood shyly by the verandah of one of the nurseries. In her hand she held a few cakes and three bananas. When she saw me she advanced gravely, presented the eatables with dignity, then, regarding me with doubtful eyes, retreated to the shelter of the good old Grannie (Devai of many a former story) who had brought her. I drew her to me, got her to sit for a moment on my knee, and answer a question or two, but only the child's sense of the mannerly held her from flight She had evidently been schooled in proper behaviour: "I will look at nothing till I have given these to Amma," she had remarked upon arrival; and now that the interview was over her one desire was to disappear and study her new world from some private corner. This was her short history:

Her mother, a good Hindu widow, had died in hospital, leaving her and a baby brother. The boy died soon afterwards, and the hospital nurse sheltered the little girl, but she had children of her own, and soon passed the child on to another woman, who was not kind to her. Then came the peril. A Temple woman nearby noticed the well-mannered child, and asked for her; again and again she asked, and she tried to attract the little girl to herself. Once the Temple woman had her she would never let her go; this was well known to the nurse. Her conscience was not very keen, but an incident only a few months old was still exerting its quickening influence within her, and she bestirred herself, wrote the post-card to us, and co-operated earnestly with Devai to get the child out of harm's way. It was not an easy matter, but with us is the Lord of hosts, and the battle for the child's soul was won. And so the little girl came to us, and written all over the quiet little face was motherlessness.

For three days that little girl followed first Devai and then one or other of the children everywhere, asking questions diligently. Where was the figure of our God? In the Temple there was a golden figure, but she had seen no figure in our church, though she had looked carefully for it. How then did we worship? A dear little girl of nine went to Paradise the day after the little new girl came, and this was an event of intense interest. Arulammal was dead, and yet we said she had gone to a happy place. How could she go anywhere when she was dead? If she were alive, what part of her was alive? Why did she smile? (the dead child's face had a tender little smile, as if she had awakened to the loveliest surprise), and so on. The questions were endless.

On the third day she suddenly woke to the sense of being loved. I was sitting on the floor in the midst of a ring of children when I felt anew little hand slipped into mine, and then suddenly the child's arms were round my neck, and she hugged and kissed me as if she had never hugged or kissed any one in all her life — which probably she hadn't; and for the rest of the evening she clung on, breaking out into kisses sometimes, and going on unmoved by the sympathetic, delighted laughter of the other children, till her hungry little heart was satisfied. "I will be good," she had whispered earnestly a little while earlier to an older child; "I will say no bad word; I will not do any- thing wrong; I will be good." It was touching to see her eager affection and to think of such a loving heart being absolutely unloved for about five years. But many a child in this sorrowful world has been unloved for five years. Not there lies the pathos of the story. Rather in this: that a child of intelligence so keen, and a nature so responsive to goodness, had so narrowly missed a fate darker and more cruel than the Christian imagination can conceive. We may try to think of such a one being trained day by day to deliberate wickedness, trained till it chooses and revels in the bad, perverted at the very spring of being; but our thoughts recoil from following far along that miry road. This, this is the tragedy of these children's lives. Not the possible suffering — some of them do not suffer at all; not the starvation where all true affection is concerned — a child may grow accustomed to starvation. The shame that burns, the wrong that stings us as we are forced to regard it, is this awful perversion of sweet to bitter, pure to vile, this deliberate defacement of the Lord's image in the soul of an innocent child.

The incident which was conducive to this little girl's emancipation is worth telling. Will any mother of young children read it unmoved?

A year ago, when the heat of March lay over the plains, a Hindu husband left his wife for a visit to Ceylon. He never returned. She had no idea whether he had died or deserted her. She and her little daughter lived on for awhile in the family house with parents-in- law and sisters-in-law, an unwelcome guest now. Then her baby was born, and still the father stayed away. So the parents-in-law sent her back to her mother in disgust, for this second baby was a girl.

Then the mother and daughter and the two little ones, following a fashion of some castes, went on pilgrimage, but the poor young wife became thinner and thinner, and at last, when they reached the town where the great Saivite Temple stands, she gave up the struggle to nurse her baby; she could no longer, she was too weak. And yet, though all round her were houses where the little one would have been welcome, and she too for its sake, she never went near them. She knew enough to know the iniquity behind those open doors. She searched till she found one whom she thought she could trust, and she laid the little babe in her arms: "See, she is dying. I cannot bear to see her die. Take her; perhaps she will live if you take her. Only promise you will never, never give her to the Temple." Not content with the verbal promise, she caused a declaration to be written and signed by the hospital nurse, in which she promised to care for the child as if she were her own, and never to give her to evil. Then having done all she could to preserve her child's life and protect her from harm, and being bound by her vow to go on, the pilgrim mother took her other little daughter's hand, and went on her weary way, content that she had saved her babe. The hospital nurse kept the little one for a month, then sold it to the Temple.

But the mother's cry had reached the open ear of God, and He, Whose tender mercies are over all His works, regarded it. One of our people heard of what had happened and wrote to us. Quickly old Devai rose and went. She arrived at the nurse's house next day, and finding the baby had really gone, and knowing full well the all but impossibility of getting it back again (for once a Temple woman has got a child, be it old or young, she holds to it with both her hands and all her might; or as it sometimes seems, the dark and awful Power to which it is to be afterwards dedicated even then lays hands upon it and grips it with a grip no human force can loosen), she was much tempted to fear lest her journey should be in vain; but round about her was that mystic vital thing, the sense of being prayed for; courageous in the consciousness of it, Devai went forward.

She found the house in an upset condition. The nurse's son, a student at a mission college, had just returned home and was indignant at what his mother had done — education helped here. He joined Devai in the protest, and together the allies brought such pressure to bear upon the Temple woman that she was forced to give the baby up. A day later she was safe in the Dohnavur nursery.

But such help as that young student gave is exceptional. When Temple Service versus Christianity is in question, there is little doubt as to which would be the choice of the greater number. "I would rather my daughter were a Temple girl than a Christian," was the open avowal of a prominent educated Hindu gentleman not long ago to one of India's Christian Governors. It is true there are exceptional men, and every now and then the Press voices an outcry against the iniquity, but the spirit behind that iniquity waits in silence, biding his time. Other interests fill the columns of our daily papers, other topics supply inspiration to eloquent orators, and the traffic in children goes on.

But the prestige attached to the profession accounts for one of our greatest difficulties in saving the children. Indirectly prestige leads to wealth. From one hundred to one hundred and fifty rupees was the price paid within the last few weeks to a young Temple woman who played and sang at a Hindu wedding in a Brahman's house in a South Indian city; so that the Temple women have it in their power to make very large offers for desirable children. This, supplemented by the influence of a depraved public opinion, accounts for the fact that there are never wanting children to "continue the succession." Still, as there is a limit to the number of available children apart from those who are kidnapped, every one saved means one less from the count, and thus apart from the indirect influence this work, as we know, exerts against the traffic, and apart from the preciousness of each little saved child, there is a satisfaction in helping to cut off the supply. May the day soon come when God Himself, in an outflash of white holiness, will deal directly with the demand.

This ease of circumstances where the more notable at least of the Temple women are concerned leads straight, as we have said, to a practical difficulty. Among the very little people, whom we call the Teddies, because they are so exactly like young delightful Teddy bears, is a small, creamy-brown person with large observing eyes. Her story illustrates this:

Some nine or ten months ago her mother, a widow, was attracted and tempted by the offer of a considerable sum of money for her six months old baby, and the usual promise of a small but sufficient endowment of land to be settled on the child if she were given up to be trained by a certain Temple woman in the service of the god inhabiting the nearest Temple to Dohnavur, the Temple with double walls and, for a country town, large establishment. The mother was flattered; that her child should be singled out by the favour of the god set upon her seemed to her something pleasant, and public opinion all round her said so too. So she went to the Temple woman's house, intending to give her the little babe then and there. The Temple woman, however, was away at a distant festival and the mother returned home. Once again she received the offer so tempting to all that was unmotherly in her, and, alas! there seems to have been much. Again her small world applauded and advised, and again she set out for the Temple woman's house. But Another had set His favour upon that little child. Once more the Temple woman was from home and the mother waited. While she was waiting, our Hindu carpenters, who lived in that town, heard of her. They told her of us, and, tired of waiting for the Temple woman and hopeful that we, being foreigners and apparently partial to this particular type of child, would rise still higher in our offer, the mother came to us.

I was in hospital with Ponnamal at the time, and could only write, "Try to hold her if you can." She had sore eyes, fortunately, and they required treatment badly; but something stronger than her faith in our medicines and desire for cure was required, and often she got impatient, and all but went. Perhaps it was prayer from the ends of the earth which kept her, for she ended in settling down to wait.

When I returned and saw the baby and heard her story I was perplexed. The little thing was most evidently desirable; we had refused several children because of the exorbitant demands made by their unnatural guardians, and those children had at once been absorbed by the neighbouring Temple. It was too impossible to send another there, and yet what the mother asked was almost equally impossible. I told her I must wait till my God told me clearly what to do. She waited a day or two longer, awed by the evidence apprehended even by her, that a Being invisible but real was in charge at Dohnavur.

On the third day directions as to what to do came, as I believed, to me. I acted upon them, and she utterly refused to listen to such a proposal as I felt free to make her. Then I told her what our God, the righteous God, would assuredly do if she sacrificed her innocent child. She departed in cold scorn, and we tightened our hold upon that little child.

Next day the mother returned. There was a kind of dread on her face: "I had to come back," she said. "What you told me your God would do He has already begun to do: I fear what He will further do." That day the papers were signed; the child was ours.

And such a child! As we look at her we often realize what a little treasure she is, and hold her with a sort of thrill of exultation in the triumph of our God. She is an interesting child apart from the interest of her story, for she is of an adventurous and most affectionate spirit; a baby of the sort no heart can refuse. She walks in at every one's door and just takes possession.

This Teddy in a temper is a pathetic object. One day I saw her toddling rapidly across some uneven ground to get to me (for Sitties and Ammal alike are the very joy of her heart). She had a rag in her hand picked up on her way. and this she waved as a flag of truce, all but tumbling over as she held it a little too far out for her still uncertain balance. Just then the small helping nurse descried her, and made for her with speed. But the Teddies can discriminate. They put small helping nurses on one platform and proper nurse Accals on quite another; on still another are perched their beloved Sitties and Ammal. This Teddy then discriminated. "Oh, it's only a small helping Accal," she must have remarked to herself, for she proceeded in my direction as fast as her fat legs could carry her. But the helping nurse, though small, was bigger than the Teddy. She overtook her and apparently suggested a return to the nursery, for I saw the Teddy suddenly sit down. The ground was rough and it must have hurt her, but more than mere hurt of body was in the howl which rose. Then the Teddy deliberately lay down on her back and kicked. The small nurse tried compulsion. The kicks grew frantic. By this time I was on the scene and peace speedily prevailed, and the Teddy meekly trotted back. Her flag had been accepted; she felt able to overlook the tyrannous behaviour of her young Accal.

Three stories; just three out of the many we could tell, but a booklet must not grow into a book, and there are dropped threads which some at least will want to pick up; so in writing as in doing, we must go on.

CHAPTER III.

PONNAMAL, AS ALL who have followed us from the Beginning know, is the brave and beloved chief sister of the Nurseries. Ponnamal, Sellamuttu, Arulai, these three form a group by themselves, and following after are a band of keen and earnest workers, Pappamal, grand-daughter of the Poet whose story is told in "Overweights of Joy," Rukma (Radiance), Preena (the Elf of "Things as They Are"), Santha (the Mouse of "Overweights "), Lavana who, as Fawn, makes a chapter in "Lotus Buds," Latha (Firefly of "Overweights " again), and Preeya, a dear little person whose happy face in a picture in "Lotus Buds" has won her many a friend. These and several others, notably Thai, another of the Poet's grand-daughters, have found their vocation on the teaching side, and little Leela, who smiles from the cover of "The Beginning," is now a helper in the kindergarten, though Leela as a teacher is as yet a too comical thought. Lola, her special chum, is on the nursing side, a bonnie young nurse in training, whose present ambition is twofold — to prove her three babies the happiest and best of all the baby family, and to turn up her hair in a knot; pigtails being, according to her ideas, unsuitable for nurses in training.

This time last year Ponnamal was very ill (cancer). Her illness, with occasional breaks for a few weeks at a time, lasted for the greater part of the year. It was an illness full of anxiety and often of keen distress, but the comforts of the Lord never failed and our hearts were refreshed in the multitude of peace. Ponnamal has been restored to us, but there were days when we walked together through the Valley of the Shadow of Death, a familiar valley now to some of us. Her restoration — or reprieve, God grant that it may prove complete restoration — has been one of the comforts of the year. She is still, however, invalided, and often in suffering, which even her brave will cannot wholly overcome.

All the Nurseries are now at Dohnavur. We found the division too difficult to continue, thankful as we were for the help of it at first; but this readers of "Lotus Buds" already know. The Nurseries owe more than words can say to the devotion of our dear Ponnamal, who first at Neyoor and then at Dohnavur, has toiled in love that never tired for the babies who are as her own to her. When she lay very ill in hospital once, I asked her what she did when she could not sleep. "I count up the children's ages," she said; "I begin with Edward Rajah" (so-called because of the resemblance to cheap prints of that monarch), "and go up to Jullanie."[3]

---

[3] Today, October 20, 1914, as I correct the proofs for this booklet, Ponnamal lies ill in the little nursery room whose picture is in "Lotus Buds." That little room, the first of all the cottage nurseries, is full of memories of joys and of sorrows, and when Ponnamal could no longer bear the noise of her own room, which opens off a larger nursery, she chose that room — the Room of Hope is its name — and so we made it ready for her. For the disease has returned and nothing human can be done to save her for us. She knows it, knows that she has the sentence of death in herself, and yet she and we all find ourselves constantly looking for the "impossible." Can it be that for the sake of our sore need — for there is no second Ponnamal — He Who eighteen months ago delivered her from so great a death will yet deliver her? But if not, Even so, Father; for so it seemeth good in Thy sight.

But at the moment of writing, with the little nursery in view, knowing that Ponnamal is waiting eagerly for the promised hour when I will go to talk over things with her, knowing that I shall find her keen over every detail concerning the children and the work, wise in every suggestion, just her own eager loving self, it is hard to believe she may be on her way to leave us. She seems so entirely alive, every faculty is as yet alive, quick and warm and vivid. Her whole thought is for us, and the devouring look of love in her great dark eyes when we go over to her or take one of her babies to see her is so strong, so living, that we turn from the thought of parting. How can we part? Will not those to whom prayer is a vital thing, pray?

Jullanie — she starts a stream of small stories, but our little bear's cub has grown into quite a decorous maiden, who learns advanced lessons and uses the English language with a certain measure of assurance. Jullanie has always been fairly correct, unlike Chellalu, who to this day throws care to the winds and pours herself out in conversation regardless of decorum as of grammar. "Amma, Amma, come look! a black one laid two white ones — not an egg, a rabbit. Went in there," continued the irrepressible child, pointing to the inner part of the hutch, into which her imagination had pursued the happy parent, "shut her eyes, laid a rabbit."

"But the Lizard is going on doing it. Lizard playing Monday songs on Sunday," this was one Sunday afternoon when her cheerful voice began to carol what I had felt bound to suggest was a Monday song:

> *The lizard runs along the ground,*
> *And then runs up a tree,*
> *It wiggle-waggles up and down*
> *And then it looks at me.*
>
> *And then it looks at me,*
> *And then it looks at me,*
> *It wiggle-waggles up and down,*
> *And then it looks at me,*

and so on to the end of a not very serious ditty. I was dragged out to the nearest tree. "There! wiggle-waggles on Sunday, going on doing Monday songs!" Bala still continues her mystic reveries, but perhaps not so frequently as formerly. "The waves are like flowers. They curl over like big flowers," she said once after gazing long at the sea; and then, "I think the sea is a Mother, she washes her children" (pointing to the rocks) "all night long." Bala used to find chronology a puzzling study. We have a decrepit old coolie called Abraham, and one day she heard him addressed by name. "Is that Abraham?" She was evidently surprised and

48

somewhat disappointed. Then after a moment's reflection, "And where is Isaac?" But she was young then.

Bala has always spiritual ideas; the scampish side of her is fairly well developed, but there is always the underlying spiritual, which her fellow-scamps respect. They were standing in a long row on the foundations of a new building one morning, waiting for the sun to rise. It was a chilly morning, and they wished he would hurry and began to advise him to do so. Presently Bala glanced down the dancing line, "He is waiting for God to tell him to come," she remarked. The line stood quiet, impressed by this remark, and the sun suddenly rose. "Now He has told him to come." Then in a flash her mood changed and the whole line broke into a shout and danced a wild dance on the edge of the wall, "Good sun! good obedient sun! "and they kissed their hands to him and salaamed, finishing off with a disrespectful shout, "Very good sun, like great big baby's ball!"

The children are as ingenious in their iniquities as ever; we sometimes wonder if anywhere there can be such outrageous children. One of our few rules is that no playthings of any sort may be taken to school. One day Sella marched a little queerly in drill. She had nothing in her hands, nothing in the wisp of blue tucked round her waist, nothing in her hair (she has a budding pigtail now in any case, and you cannot tuck away many things in pigtails). At last she was stopped and called out of the line, and, adjured to confess, disclosed four large seeds fitted between her five toes. It is something sometimes to be barefoot. And another day Nesa Sittie, who was trying to get a little quiet between a noon class and early afternoon school, was stirred past endurance by what sounded like numerous cats performing all at once. She called a child from the nearest nursery from which the catawauling proceeded, and was told that Rachel Accal had put Preetha, Sarala, Nundinie, and Manorama (Puck No. 2) in the middle of the room as a punishment (corners being places where much mischief may be done), because they had gathered and eaten tamarind flowers and were likely presently to have pains, and the middle of the room was a safe and easy place to find them when, as was probable, they would require attention. The five in the meantime were feeling well and happy, and had relieved the monotony of life by holding their noses tight and then singing at the tops of their voices. Chellalu and Evu have a quieter way of dealing with punishments: put one or other out of her class, for incorrigible idleness or any other sin, she immediately and gratefully sleeps. And Nundinie (Dimples, she used to be) has a way of her own which takes the sting out of admonitions: "Forgive me, Lord," she said unexpectedly at the end of yesterday's prayer, "and change my dear, naughty, nice disposition."

We can only console ourselves, as we meditate on these things, by the remark made in a letter from a friend well acquainted with the genus child, in its many varying species, and head of a great Indian educational work: "I don't think yours are worse than others," she said kindly, "only they let you know what is in them, which ours don't always." They certainly do.

We do not belong to Government, and are therefore uninspected; but once, two years or so ago, before we had the advantage of experienced help in our school, we were visited by a proper school inspector. The kindergarten was respectful but perplexed. Questions of a sort calculated to draw the youthful mind were asked, and Pappamal was a little anxious; she knew what might happen, for she had inquired once of a well-taught class, "Which pair of the rabbit's legs are the longer?" and been assured solemnly, "Those which are long are longer." Her class, however, survived the ordeal, and beyond being weak in sums did nothing dreadful. Preena's, which contains Tara, Evu, and children of that size, sinned worst. "How many lions are there in that picture?" "Three." "And how many legs have they each got?" "Four." "Altogether how many legs have the three lions got?" The answer for a wonder was correct. "Good children! Now why have they got twelve legs?" But this was too much. "To walk with," was the unanimous and emphatic reply. It was worse when he came to geography. This subject is not usually taught to small children in India, and the inspector doubted their being fit for it, so he began low: "What is that?" pointing to a lake on a raised map. "It is a lake." "What is in a lake?" The whole class gasped. Several of their elders an evening or two before had looked in the microscope and seen some of the inhabitants of a drop of water. There had not been time for these smaller people to see the wonders, but they had been impressed and perhaps a little confused by the excited descriptions of the entranced observers. "I see a bell, five bells. − Oh, they have tails, no, corkscrews − the corkscrews are shooting up − now they are straight. Oh, the bells are alive!" Or still more mysterious, "Oh, a wheel! now it's whirring − it's a head, no, a wheel and it's alive!" Which did the worthy inspector want, vorticella or rotifer? Neither, apparently, for when they ventured upon echoes of the above he did not seem satisfied at all. "Fishes," hazarded a hopeful child, but even that fell flat. Afterwards, when they were told he had wanted them to say water, they gazed in mute amazement, and a "well, you can never tell what is in the grown-up mind" kind of air. The inspector was quite sure they were too young to learn geography.

He would have been still more firmly riveted in his ideas if he had known the K.G. view of the people on the other side of the world. They are much to be pitied when it rains on our side, for the rain soaks through to them and wets their houses, which being upside down, must be in a most uncomfortable condition when soaking wet inside. The Sittie thus informed − the matter was treated as quite natural and simple − began to expound things a little, but was met by a discomfiting "I do not understand it in the least." For there are limits to a child's power of understanding, though none whatever to its powers of imagination, and blessedly, none to its faith. The wise grown-up person sometimes forgets this, though all day long and every day the children keep on reminding us, so that we really need not forget.

Their powers of imagination: sometimes we wonder if we shall ever get to the end of these quaint imaginings. Heaven is rich in animal life, the donkeys are white there, and little children ride on them. "And there are cats there, gold cats," this was Sarala; and later, by way of further information, "In Heaven the frogs are gold." And there are pumas there, as we shall hear later. The electric torch is illuminated by means of fireflies inside. Welsh mountains are well-washed mountains. Manx cats suggest a new joy: "Then we can put on knickers. If there is a tail it gets in the way." As to matters of ordinary life, it is obvious that the sun does not really set in the sea, though he appears to do so, "for if the sun did go into the sea we could not bathe, the water would be too hot." This was Sarala again, Pickles of "Lotus Buds," and was after all not so much imagination as sensible inference; more than one might have expected from Pickles, who, as her unfortunate teacher remarks, "does not value learning," by which she means lessons. A brilliant suggestion whereby a Sittie might avoid going away on furlough was, she might sit in a tree, up among the branches: "You can come down when you are strong." The vision of a Sittie sitting patiently for months up a tree, the densest shade of which is unsafe in the heat of the day, was just wild enough to be pleasant. And so it is all the time; irrational, delightful, ever refreshing is the real inside mind of a child.

But it has its bewilderments. If we find ourselves puzzled at times by revelation of far distances, or pulled up suddenly as we knock up against some unexpected limitation, how much more must the child be puzzled when she discovers the unexpected in us; fathomless knowledge is ours she knows, but sometimes undoubtedly she comes across amazing ignorance. This was quite perfectly expressed one day by Sella, who ran up to her Prema Sittie holding a yellow *thevetia* flower in her hand. "Sittie, what is the name of this flower?" But Premie Sittie had specialized upon severer things than flowers, and she said, "I don't know; ask Ammal." Whereupon Sella, surprised out of her customary politeness, and gazing up dauntlessly to her five-foot-seven-inches-tall Sittie, delivered her soul in English: "You know all about B.A., and you don't know the name of this flower! "

But our strange way of looking at common, evident, uncontestable things is the most unaccountable part of us. The big tamarind-tree, for example; we regard it chiefly as a nice, shady place where children can play on the safe downstairs of the world, as it were, without danger of injury to life or limb. To the children, on the other hand, the tamarind is chiefly valuable because of its glorious upstairs. Up among those branches are forked seats, overlooking the lower sphere, and there are secret holes up there where treasures can be stowed away. That, not its mere shade on the flat expanse of sand below, is its chief value. And the swings: it may be all very well to swing up and down in the ordinary way, but that is nothing to the joys of a twirl. Twist the ropes just as tight as you possibly can, your prostrate body face downwards across the seat, then suddenly let the ropes unwind — a dizzy spin is the result, and could anything be so rapturous? But grown-up people do not see it. They think the mad spin perilous and bad for the rope, and are terribly unimaginative and unsympathetic on the whole subject.

But we are forgiven everything and loved notwithstanding our shortcomings: "Where is Premie Sittie?" It was Rutnie, who used to be Huffs, who asked Piria Sittie the question. Piria Sittie told her Premie Sittie's whereabouts, adding, "What do you want her for?" "To love her," was Rutnie's reply — a rather sweet one, if you come to think of it. Has not even a dull grown-up sometimes found herself wanting somebody for no particular purpose but just to love her?

Still, I do not want to represent the Lotus Buds as by any means immaculate innocents. This, from a person called Varatha, is sufficient, I think, to dispel any such mistaken notion. Mr. Beath, Premie Sittie's father, called by the children Partiya (Grandfather), was with us at the time of the story, and the occasion was his kind, frequently pressed invitation to her to sit on his knee at tea-time. She always shook her head decidedly; she preferred her own high chair. One evening, however, she relented a little. "Tomorrow," she remarked in Tamil, "tomorrow I will sit on your knee." Tomorrow came and she was reminded of her promise, but declined to keep it. This was serious. Promises, even babies' promises, are sacred things; but Varatha seemed untroubled by pricks of conscience, and smilingly assured us she would do it "tomorrow." Next day I met her walking down the garden-walk on her way to tea. "Don't forget your promise, Varatha; you said you would sit on Partiya's knee." Varatha looked up in my face, and her expression was quite inscrutable. "Tomorrow," she answered serenely. "I said tomorrow; this is today" Whether she was puzzled by the changeful ways of words, or whether she was just "doing us," I do not know. Naturally she never explained.

And yet there is another side to Varatha. She was nearly three and a half when a little playfellow, Lulla, passed from our happy play down here to the happier Play of Paradise; but so far as we had seen she had not thought much about it, just taking the event for granted as a natural, and for Lulla very pleasant, thing, in the way little children do so blessedly accept the happenings of life. But she must have thought; for one evening she was found running excitedly among the bushes in the garden. "Sittie, Sittie, look!" Areenie Sittie stooped to the child's level and looked. There was no general glory in the sky, but just where Varutha could see it a rift of sunset gold had broken through,

"What is it, Varutha?" "Lulla, Heaven!" explained Varutha, sure of being understood. Thus, day by day, apart from us and our clumsy ways and words, the little child is taught in a speech and in a language that it can understand.

The friendships of our small children continue to be as full of tragedy and comedy as ever. Tara and Evu, however, have not been quite so devoted of late as they used to be. But it was some time before Tara would admit the fact. She thought it too unkind.

Once Tara broke her arm. How she managed it no one knew, for she was swinging on a low swing at the time, and need not have done it. However, she did it, and Evu's distress was as great as Tara's. While it was being set by the village bone-setter — a prolonged and painful experience (but he is clever in his way, and the fracture was simple) — Evu hovered round like an agitated mother bird over an injured nestling. And her pride in Tara was great. Tara did not cry. Months afterwards Prema Sittie broke her wrist, and her subsequent heroic conduct was the talk of the family. Evu alone refused to flatter. "Tara very little; Tara not cry. Prema Sittie very Goliath, why [should] she cry?" Night and day, till Tara had quite recovered, Evu was her faithful slave. If Tara woke at night Evu was up in an instant — she insisted on sleeping beside her on my verandah, for she was "Tara's friend." The bone-setter was much struck by this devotion, and he admired Evu with an admiration second only to his feelings for Tara, "an excellent child, a child of much patience," as he told her once to her face, to her undisguised pleasure. "A very good man," she remarked approvingly after his departure that day, and quite looked forward to his daily visits. As, indeed, so did I, for that bone-setter is another Yosepu for quaintness. He has only one good eye — the other differs in texture and expression from the good one; and this, combined with his extraordinary collection of wrinkles, adds to his impressiveness as he squats beside his patient and discourses upon his other patients. "There was one, an old man of seventy, and his family called me in alarm, for he had a compound fracture" (this was not the word he used; his word was really a gruesomely detailed description of the appearance of the unhappy arm). "But fractures, compound fractures, or any sort of fractures, are small matters to me. You lay hold of the bone which sticks out, so" (illustrating with one grimy hand), "and you pull, so" (and another gesture only too vivid showed it all), "and then you just push and pull and push and pull till you get the jagged bit in again." "Do you wash your hands before you do all this?" "Before? No," with a glance of pity at such simplicity. "But after- wards I wash them, for they get all bloody."

They used to be in different classes, Tara and Evu; Tara was usually top of her class, and Evu bottom of hers. One day Evu got to the top by accident. The question which gave her the chance of her life was, "What comes out of a butterfly's egg?" "Caterpillar," said Evu, who had seen it do it, and she went up top. For weeks she remained in that proud position, but only because the rest of the class at that time were exceedingly slack, and not because of any virtue in Evu. This easily retained pre-eminence began to have a bad effect on her soul, so she was removed into Tara's class, where it was not so easy to be top.

At first this plan worked well. Tara naturally was overjoyed and danced about, kissing Evu at intervals in the rapture of her loving little heart. Evu looked like a shy boy under these embraces, but really seemed to try to rise towards Tara's heights, and by dint of good fortune did actually rise. It was all Tara could do to refrain herself from telling Evu the answer to such questions as would bring her up farther; once she certainly missed in order, as Preena divined, to let Evu up, and as she went down herself, she turned and beamed on Evu, and patted her approvingly.

But this happy state of things was short-lived. Gradually the foolish pride of emulation waxed faint in Evu's breast and she sank slowly, followed by Tara, who seemed to slide down on purpose. One day Evu was banished to a lower class as incorrigibly idle. "Never mind, Evu," Tara was overheard remarking, "I will be naughty too, and then Preena Accal will turn me out too, and we will both sit at the bottom and play."

This embarrassing comradeship lasted till one day when a fit of more than usual impishness seized Evu, and Tara removed herself from her. At present they are friendly doubtless underneath, but on the surface a little cool, and their Nurse Accal, the faithful Esli, observes with thankfulness that Tara does at least sometimes assert her independence and refuse to follow Evu into scrapes.

With the advent of two whole Sitties for the school side, things have gradually grown more scholastic though not less cheerful in the K.G., or rather what is now a transition school where mature people of nine and ten and eleven have "zaminations" and do occasionally take things seriously, as we lately unexpectedly proved. For a week or so ago, when our Collector and his wife were seeing over the school and nurseries, we were arrested by the extraordinary gravity of the A and B classes, classes generally inclined to frivolity and by no means depressed in behaviour. Not a child would speak above a whisper, not one smiled. This was altogether so unlike their usual school behaviour that we passed on considerably puzzled by the unwonted sobriety of life in the A class-room, and inclined to apologize for what we could not understand. That evening a communicative group composed of A's and B's poured information upon us: "We were doing Zamination" ("*Ex*amination" corrected several at once) "and it was very difficult, and we thought we would lose all our marks" (marks having superseded place in class). "And how could we speak, and how could we be happy, when in each of our eyes there was a tear, and we had to hold it there, like this" — and an eye screwed up and stiffened showed how it was accomplished. Then there was a war-whoop and a war-dance, which if only he could have seen it, doubtless would have interested the kind Collector Durai considerably more than did the unnaturally care-weighted students. "Now play polar bear!" and the episode ended in raids and rushes, and tears held carefully in eyes were things of the far past.

As in earlier days, so now, the Scriptures and hymns continue to provide material for innumerable excursions into the land some of us love to walk in, the land of new ideas, on the borders of the children's world. One day last April it was too hot to be hungry. It was holiday time, and the A's and B's had accompanied us to dinner. But dinner was impossible: "That is right," remarked Chellalu approvingly, as the everlasting chicken was discarded with the impious wish that some other species of animal were obtainable, "yes, that is right: food is vain. There was a prophet and the Lord God told him not to eat any bread or drink any water but go straight home. And he ate bread and he drank water and a lion ate him." The Book of Ecclesiastes was at that time the Children's Scripture Reading portion, and many were the reflections suggested by the meditations of the king. "This" (the kindergarten room) "is a mere henhouse, and that" (pointing out to one of the cottages) "is a mere henhouse, and all here," a comprehensive sweep of the arm included the whole compound, "is a mere henhouse. But Heaven"

Words failed her at this point and she looked up rapturously. At such moments Chellalu appears what she is not, almost angelic. But even Chellalu has her moments of spiritual illumination; it was she who said, speaking of Enoch, "God called him, and he went"; and it was the same mad-cap child who, in telling the story of the entry into Jerusalem, thus paraphrased the words of our Lord: "If the children do not sing, the stones will walk and sing to Me."

Still apropos of the vanity of earthly things was this: We may not lay up treasure on earth. "All earthly things are vain; this pencil-box" (waving it) "is vain. When we die, burn it all up!" "I suggested," says the Sittie, "it would be better to leave our Bibles and pencil-boxes for other children." The Scamp agreed: "Yes, for the heathen children. My Bible is nicely marked, very useful for heathen children." This from Chellulu, of all people, was really striking. If only she lived according, what a treasure she would be! Her ideas, however, as to the way to convert the world outside the compound are, it is to be feared, somewhat crude, and like most of her plans, drastic. This, for example, explains her fairly lucidly: "You break all the idols and then the heathen are much afraid, and they say, 'Oh no! Oh no! we will worship the true God.'" Varied by, "God will send an earth-shake in that place and break all the idols very nicely, and the people [will] say, 'Oh! oh! we are very sorry; we won't do it anymore.'"

"Able from these stones to raise up children unto Abraham" was the amazing sentence which riveted attention one day lately. Nesa Sittie was the teacher. "Can God make anything into children?" Nesa Sittie said it was even so. Seela's eyes traversed the classroom. There is a huge blackboard there, much bigger than blackboards usually are. Seela fixed upon this big black thing and pointing to it inquired, "God can make that blackboard a child?" Nesa Sittie could only say, "Yes, if He wished to He could." But Seela had found something still more unpromising, a picture of a shiny seal on a slab of ice. "And the seal?" Nesa Sittie assured her He certainly could if He wished. But she was not sorry to return to more ordinary subjects, for the transformation of blackboards and seals into children was only too evidently being visualized by at least five of the attentive six present in that Bible-class, and children richly endued with a sense of the comic can do terrible things when too far tried. Seela, however, reverted to the subject more than once, and not long ago remarked impressively out of school hours: "Do you know that God can make blackboards and seals into children — if He wishes?"

Things on both sides the Unseen are extremely vivid. The sermon one Sunday had been on David and Jonathan, and Pyarie, discussing it, said she loved Jonathan best. To a suggestion that she loved the Lord Jesus best she paused to consider, then continued, "I love the Lord Jesus much, much, much. Then I love Jonathan much, next David, next Solomon. I do not love one best, that is Sasu" (the Devil). The drop into Tamil, and mutilated Tamil too, for *Pisasu* is the name of the person to whom Pyarie had referred, tickled Sella, and she laughed. Why had Pyarie dropped the "Pi"? But Pyarie had a sufficient reason: her name began with Pi; therefore she left that first syllable out when speaking of the unbeloved. The two children were in Nesa Sittie's room at the time and continued chattering, presently remarking, in mixed Tamil and English, that they would not like to live in that room, it had two doors, and a snake might come in by one door and a robber by the other. As it happened a big lizard (bloodsucker is its rather gruesome common name) had fixed upon the stone pillar supporting the roof as a suitable residence, but their Sittie reminded them of the One who was wherever His children were, to which Sella assented, "Yes, bloodsucker stays here to bite" (a mistake, the creature is innocent), "God stays to take care." A comfortable view of things which satisfied them both. The direct, if abbreviated, language often points a story, as when part of our Lord's temptation was thus summarized: "Satan told a big lie; he said, 'I made all this; if you bow Me I will give it to you!'" And rich words come to the rescue sometimes and help out the meagre store, as when Thai Accal slew an insect and a small child kindly excused her: "Accal does not know the preciousness of that puchie."

And the hymns. Indian children have no difficulty in understanding things spiritually, but occasionally a literal translation of their thoughts, so to speak, is permitted. One evening Seela was looking at a picture of a puma. She duly discovered for herself that it was self-coloured, the only large cat except the lion not striped like a tiger or spotted like the leopard. "Good puma," was the unexpected observation, and she began to croon to herself "There is a city bright," till she got to the line "spotless and stainless, spotless and stainless," when she stopped to stroke the puma. "Many pumas in heaven." But as usual it was Chellalu who did the thing most thoroughly. The Christmas hymn was floating in her head, apparently, for about Christmas time she rushed into the schoolroom in blissful excitement: "Look! oh, look! Where a mother laid her baby!" and she held out a large green leaf, in the middle of which was a small white patch, a bit of silk fluff, and out of it was crawling a spider.

Spiders are a continual interest, sometimes half shuddery but sometimes most comfortable. There was one who made her web exactly across the one of the schoolroom windows so that the children could conveniently watch her avocations. It happened to be our rainy season, and regularly before rain that intelligent animal used to run down her line, roll up her web into a ball and tuck it under the window eave, so that it was never destroyed by the rain. Trap-door spiders are among the wonders of our compound, but only once have we found the silk door with its hinge complete. This treasure was covered by a finger-glass in hope of protecting it, but a miserable crow saw the finger-glass, upturned it, and presumably ate the silken door, for we never saw it again. The children's delightful familiarity with living things has occasionally led into peril, as when Evu brought a yellow scorpion in her half-closed little hand, purring to it softly: "Pretty puchie!" But the ablest of the guardian angels was surely on duty the day the B class saw a cobra for the first time. A deputation scampered across for me to come and look at the marvellous snake which "stood up and made an arch"; a graphic gesture showed me the spread hood and waving head, and I fled out to find a circle of admirers round a large cobra which Seela, whose sympathies are as yet sadly undeveloped, was pretending to hit over the head with a stick. The cobra, enraged, but mercifully for the moment paralysed, perhaps by the audacity of the small humans, was swaying to and fro, hood outspread, the tongue flicking in and out. Blessed be the guardian angels upon whose assistance we do most sincerely count, for we are very short of nurses; but blessed, most blessed, be the Lord of all the angels, Whose face the good angels do ever behold on behalf of these little ones committed to their care.

CHAPTER IV.

THE COMPOUND — that mere but delightful henhouse — has grown considerably since "The Beginning" was written. It includes now several acres, covered more or less, or being covered, with nurseries and other scattered little buildings; for we have no massing of children together, and their free life in the good fresh air accounts, we think, for much of their usually good health and riotous spirits. Each cottage is surrounded by a trellis both for privacy and for beauty, and the climbers, jessamine, antigone, thunbergia, morning glory and other varieties of convolvulus are among the joys of the children's lives. The trellises sometimes serve other uses, as, for example, last Sunday, when a small girl, sent from her nursery in disgrace as too tiresomely unruly ("She doesn't want to do anything she ought," was the complaint), spent a solitary salutary hour in searching for a disobedient jessamine. Later in the day she was overheard describing her experience: "And I could not find one. For God had said to the jessamine, 'Your leaves must grow one opposite the other'; and they did. Sometimes I found one where there was no opposite leaf, but there was a little thing" (leaf bud she meant) "opposite, so there had been a leaf, only it had fallen off. No, I could not find one disobedient jessamine!"

These little nursery rooms are very dear to their owners. The pictures, the best we can get, are possessed with a happy sense of possession, and very minutely studied. The little teakwood book- shelves let into the walls, the very tiles on the floor which they most diligently scrub, are their "sonthum," their own. All this helps towards the family feeling which is such a marked feature of our happy Dohnavur life. My fellow-workers are Sitties to them all, (Sittie means mother's younger sister, which with one exception the Sitties are), and the Accals are sisters in truth. Each who is fit for it has charge of a nursery. Sundoshie (the young wife whose people tried three times to poison her) and Esli are perhaps the only two whose names would be familiar to readers of this story. But among the nurses in training are those whom some will remember. Karuna (the Duckling of "Things"), for example, and even little Tingalu, for whom the devoted Yosepu still entertains a high regard. This small person is a helper to the helping nurses — a very junior position, but she will rise in time.

Many have been the inquiries about the worthy Yosepu, so a word about him may not be out of place. He continues entirely affectionate, but has lately been considering the question of marriage, and this has had a somewhat disturbing effect upon him. He has become a little hazy about his duties, and sometimes forgets them. But he is as interesting as ever. One day about Christmas time a parcel of toys came from home, and he was in the room when they were unpacked. I left the room for a moment, and when I returned Yosepu was on his knees holding in his clasped hands a small black furry animal. His eyes were turned devotionally up; his whole expression, every wrinkle in him, was twisted into an appeal for that black animal. Who could have resisted him? I could not. So the doll in pink silk has a companion now.

The monotony — never too monotonous — of life at Dohnavur is interrupted by expeditions to the foothills on Saturday afternoons, when the patient Areenie Sittie crowds herself into a bandyful of children and allows herself to be tumbled over three hot miles of execrable road to the foot of our great rock. Then the bandy pours out its excited contents, and everybody roams and scrambles about till, too soon, it is time to return. On the way certain idols have to be passed; the order of the day then is for one or more small girls to lay hands upon Sittie's face with an earnest, "Turn your face round, Sittie; don't look at the sad thing." Once a bandy load of children passing a little idol temple began suddenly to sing; "For God to hear and not be sorry," they explained. Sometimes a break of another kind occurs and we have Cooley days, when everyone puts on a cooley turban and does real cooley work with uncooley-like energy. "Give me thirty of the children and I will get sixty cooleys' work done for you," once remarked the long-tried Sellamuttu, who at that time was engaged in superintending cooleys; but we cannot always spare thirty, for lessons have to be learned in the intervals of other things. Still, we have cooley days frequently enough to keep the compound in fairly good order, and the effect of such days upon the children is excellent. And finally we still have our Coming Day Feasts, days of delight to the garlanded children, who sit now not in little rows as of old, but in many circles on the floor of the big Praise Room in the kindergarten.

The compound, like the family, has been growing of late. A new field .has been included, and our expectation is to have twelve little nurseries, to be called by the names of the twelve precious stones. But we cannot speak of expectations without the question rising, Who is responsible for all this expenditure? So perhaps it is well to say at once that no one on earth is responsible for us. The C.E.Z. Keswick, Messrs. Morgan and Scott, Messrs. Marshall Brothers, and our Home Secretary, pass on whatever they receive for us, but no one is responsible for our supplies. And yet never once have they failed.

And again it needs to be said clearly that no one is authorized to ask for money for us. We have three reasons for this decision: we do not wish to risk doing others the wrong of receiving what, if we had not asked for it, might have gone to them. We do not want to have the responsibility of spending anything which we cannot be quite sure was intended for us; and we have found it enough to ask our Heavenly Father. That second reason may read a little obscurely, but to us at least it is simple enough.

Expenditure leads out into expenditure; the only expenditure, with all its outworkings, for which God can be held to be responsible is that which He directs. The spending of money in the first instance, therefore, is a serious business, and we do not want to take to ourselves this responsibility. In other words, we do not want to have more money to spend than we are authorized to use. A gift given at the request of a friend might or might not be His intention for us. It is conceivable, at least, that it might not. He might have meant it for someone else when our kind friend intercepted it. But about money unasked except in prayer can there be any such doubt? and is not all that is involved in using it to open new work, or to extend old work, assured to us in the initial gift which we accept as an earnest of the whole?

So we continue as we began, asking only the One in Whose hand are all supplies, and the oil in the cruse does not fail. As we pour it out it comes. It is very simple but at times very awesome, for it brings the Lord our Master near and causes us afresh to recognize Him as practically, not just theoretically, in charge. "He hath shamed me with His kindness": the words are written on the fly-leaf of my account-book, and no words could more truly tell the story of the years. I have said all this before elsewhere, but can it be said too often or too clearly? For the age is full of question, and do not such answers as these, direct, actual, supply an answer to at least one of the most persistent? There is no myth, no imagination about it: God does hear when we speak to Him; God does answer us. For money is a tangible, unmistakable thing; you cannot act when you have not got it as you would it you had it. It is not a case of "Believe that you have it, and you have it" — a kind of faith which has puzzled me from a child. Believe it will come, yes, if you are sure your order is to go forward and buy land or build buildings or save children. But woe unto you if you imagine you have been told to do such things and then find the order has not been signed above. But the sign, the very impress of the signet ring, when you are inwardly assured that you will see it and do see it, is a solemn thing to see; then indeed you are silent in the Presence: you can only adore. And when the blessed money comes, and you handle it, you see an invisible mark upon every coin, and oh how earnestly you seek for the attentive ear to catch the lightest tone of that Voice which alone must direct the spending of it.

Ponnamal's great desire now is a well with a *kamalai*, a device worked by two bullocks by which water is drawn for the watering of a large field. This field she already sees converted into a flourishing vegetable garden, where all the needs of the ever-growing family will be met, without the present daily difficulty of sending out to search the countryside for vegetables. And the teaching Sitties' castle in the air is a suitable school, apart from the kindergarten, which will then be left to the possession of the babies large and small. That this is, and may be for some time to come, a castle in the air does not trouble us at all; for, as Mr. Benson tells us, Bishop Westcott reproved the scoffer who laughed at castles in the air, by asking him where else they could be built, "If they are not built in the air they will be of the earth earthy." So we build ours first in the air.

Thus the life that we live at Dohnavur is in the true sense of the word care-less. We are not careful for the provision of our needs. We are only careful lest we grieve the Spirit who directeth us, by any unholiness of walk or character, or by any mistake as to His purposes. We are often grateful that financial burdens are never allowed to press, for of cares and anxieties of other kinds we have many. Is it that our Father, knowing this, and knowing that it must be so, sends our little ones (who are first of all His little ones, which accounts for everything, does it not?) their rice and curry and blue seeleys and all else, as it were, apart from us and our exertions, so that we have not to use our strength in wresting money from shut- up purses (a thing we could never do), but in wresting souls from the grasp of the evil one, the poor little prey from the Terrible, leaving to His kind attention the matter of supplies.[4]

And truly few weeks pass without a fight of some kind and a burden on the spirit. Sometimes the fight is of a sort that, thank God, comes but rarely, when we have to live through experiences which cannot wisely be written down and printed. Some things in work like ours have to be locked up in silence. Sometimes, again, it is just the ordinary fight, the struggle which never can grow easier to save the children appointed to death. In a booklet called "From Dohnavur" the story is told of such a child. Similar stories are being lived out in many a house in Southern India. But the end is not always as it was with that noble child; oftener the poor little crushed girl gives in. I heard of one such only last week. "She is entirely changed. She fled to us twice and begged us to protect her, but we could do nothing. She was seized and carried off and garlanded, and the thing was done. When we saw her a few weeks later, her face was evil and hard." These are the heart-breaks of this life. We look at our own bright children, and they look straight in our eyes as English children look; they have not a particle of that furtive, conscious expression so often seen in a land where childhood ends almost as soon as it begins. We know the children through and through, know their naughtiness, wilfulness; know enough to make us pray with a fervency mothers will understand, "O God, save them through and through, or take them quickly to Thyself!" Know, too, their innocence, dearness, lovableness; know how straight and clear they are, how responsive to the good. Many of them do truly seem to turn naturally to the good, rejoicing in it, and loving it with a

---

[4] This was written before the War began; we are beset by new circumstances now. But even so the Covenant stands fast: "Let no anxieties fret you." Mr. Arthur Way's translation of Phil. 4:6 is a word of quietness for these strange and difficult days.

sweet, earnest love. The Lord Jesus is real to them; in their childish way they are His little lovers. Then we think of these others who might have been as they, now "evil and hard." Oh the pity of it, and the shame!

CHAPTER V.

SOMETIMES, AS IF to accentuate it all, God seems to stoop and take one of our little ones and perfect her, as if to show how beautiful a thing His intention is, that we may more ardently press on, and save more to become His fair handiwork in the days to come. One such was Lulla, the little one who found a place in "Lotus Buds" beside Dimples, who is now a kindergartener of much distinction; but Lulla is learning elsewhere. Her little life, in spite of frequent illnesses, was one bright summer's day. She had a delicate infancy, but seemed to be growing healthy, and we had begun to expect to keep her. She was five when, as the Psalm for the day she was taken puts it, the angels were given charge over her to keep her in all her ways, even the new untried way which leads to Paradise: "They shall bear thee in their hands" — the words come to us so comfortingly month by month as the day returns — "that thou hurt not thy foot against a stone." Even the dear little feet would be the angels' care in that new journey.

Lulla was just a loving, sweet-tempered, intelligent child, prettier perhaps than any other child here, for she was a beautiful north - country Brahman. She delighted in her kindergarten plays and lessons, and she and Dimples were inseparable, a charming little pair. They had opened their affection to admit Neela, a small girl of their own age, a flower-like little creature with a story behind her of battle and triumph, which rejoiced our hearts every time we saw her at play with the other dear little two. They were a pretty trio, "fair" as the word goes in the South; dainty, delightful little beings.

One day — it was August 15, 1912 — Lulla was not very well. We were not very anxious; she had been often ill and had pulled through. But she rapidly grew worse. We wired for help; it arrived an hour too late. For on the third morning a glance told us the truth. Oh the pang of such a moment! I went straight from her to Ponnamal's little back room and prayed that she might be taken. It was too much to see that sweet, patient child suffer as she was suffering then.

When I returned to the nursery where her Piria Sittie and Ponnamal Accal were watching her, they told me she had been smiling. I hardly believed it. I thought it was one of those little delusions which can come at such times. But to hear a trained hospital nurse, and one not given to delusions, say it, was unexpected. Suddenly, as I watched, the child smiled unmistakably, a radiant, eager smile, then flung her arms out and up and clapped her hands just as she had often done when one of us came into the nursery. It was just that, nothing else; a gesture of quick, delighted surprise and welcome. She did it again, looking up eagerly and smiling all over her face; then she turned, flung her arms round my neck, then round her Sittie's, and kissed us good-bye. Ponnamal was sitting at her feet and she did not seem to see her, but the good-bye to us was as unmistakable as the smile. Out went her little hands again as if asking to be lifted up. She seemed eager to be off, and we felt as we looked, if such rapture can be granted to a child of five years old, what must the rapture of the ripe saint be? And still we watched, awed. If all three of us had not seen it we should have doubted its reality; as it was we cannot doubt

Jesus, tender Shepherd, hear me,
Bless Thy little lamb tonight,
Through the darkness be Thou near me,
Keep me safe till morning light.

Through the darkness — there was only another minute or two of it, hardly time enough to sing, as best we could, her hymn to her, and then that radiant, wonderful smile passed and she was gone. Gone, but alive, conscious, rejoicing; we knew it: we could not doubt it. What had she seen? Whom had she seen? We who had watched her felt as if the veil had been drawn aside: we had looked in.

Friends, shall we not continue? Can we do otherwise than continue? Could we shut our nursery doors because of inevitable difficulties, and say "Enough — let the Temples have the rest of the children"? We cannot say it; we cannot imagine ourselves ever saying it. We must save more Lullas, more and more. Help us, then, to continue.

CHAPTER VI.

BUT THE FUTURE — "What are you going to do with them all in the future?" This is the inevitable second question, and it is asked sometimes with real concern, sometimes with a shade of gentle reproof in it, as if the questioner almost wondered if we ever gave the matter a thought, little knowing it is never far from us. Sometimes it haunts us, and frightens us, and sends us in desperation to our knees: "Lord, thou art Lord of the future. It cannot be too difficult for Thee!"

"She lives in a Utopia," was the encouraging remark made to one of us lately at home on furlough, with regard to me and my present And another, with equal knowledge of facts, rose to the cheerful heights of, "I pity her, I pity her with all my heart when I think of all that is before her when her children grow up!" Neither of these sanguine sympathizers nor one out of the hundred questioners has any idea of how their doubts appeal to the anxious, cowardly part of us, for —

Far in the future
Lieth a fear,
Like a long low mist of grey,
Gath'ring to fall in a dreary rain.
Thus doth thy heart within thee complain,
And even now thou art afraid, for round, thy dwelling
The flying winds are ever telling
Of the fear that lieth grey,
Like a gloom of brooding mist upon the way.

Thank God, there is another word waiting to be said:

But the Lord is always kind,
Be not blind,
Be not blind
To the shining of His face,
To the comforts of His grace;
Hath He ever failed thee yet?
Never, never; wherefore fret?
Oh, fret not thyself, nor let
Thy heart be troubled,
Neither let it be afraid.

And still another:

Nearby thy footfall
Springeth a joy
Like a new-blown little flower
Growing for thee, and to make thee glad;
Let thy countenance be no more sad,
But wake the voice of joy and health within thy dwelling,
And may thy tongue be ever telling
Not of fear that lieth grey,
But of springing flowers of joy beside thy way.

These verses express something of our feelings as we look past today into tomorrow. It is true that tomorrow may never come, but all the same it is our business to prepare for it, and one way surely is to be of a grateful, hopeful spirit and to refuse to shut our eyes to the blessings of today. He Who has been with us today, planting flowers by our roadside, will be with us tomorrow. What is now our present was once future to us. Perhaps the mists we saw in the time now past, as we looked across with fearful hearts into that which today is our present, may have watered the roots of these flowers of delight. But be the worst that can be awaiting us, nevertheless the Lord is kind, He has never failed us yet; why then should we fret and let our hearts be troubled? And may we not conclude that if it is right to save the children in the first instance — and who doubts it now? — help will come when they grow up? Will not the One to Whom we always look as alone responsible, undertake the future when it comes — if it comes — for is He not the God of the future as much as of the present? I say if it comes, for at least some of us are hastening unto the Coming of the Lord in glad anticipation. But if that Coming be delayed and the difficult future has to be lived through, even so, need we, should we fear?

It is worse than useless to blind our eyes to facts. The work could not have been started in a more unpromising, difficult place, so far as the future for the girls is concerned. Tinnevelly is the last place in India where one would have chosen to start such a colony, and this for reasons pressing enough to force themselves upon us. But who started the work? Who chose the place? From the point of view of the present it is perfect. The children could hardly have been kept in safety had we been near a city. Surely, then, the choice of place may be left in peace. The future was present to the One who chose Dohnavur for us, when He chose it.

But so far, though we are now surrounded by growing up and grown up girls, as well as by little children, we have not felt our need of pity, for we have found very many flowers. One by one our older girls have become keen and willing helpers, and some of them have refused offers of marriage that they might give themselves to the absorbing work of helping to care for the little ones. Years ago a notable missionary in South India proposed starting something in the line of a Sisterhood or a Deaconess Home, where the more earnest Indian girls conscious of a vocation might find what English girls can so readily find, a welcome, and shelter, and guidance. But nothing of the sort in the least appealed to me. I feared anything in the nature of vows, expressed or understood. Nor did India seem ready for it. But some at least of our girls appear to be choosing the life of freedom to attend upon the Lord without distraction. When I rather pressed one lately to reconsider her decision, she brought me I Cor. 7:34; and certainly in this part of the East, as things are at present, there is extraordinary force in the remark. But we never let any of the girls bind herself in spirit, and the satisfactory marriage of some of the earlier converts is always quotable on the side of the ordinary life. So far, however, to the immense help of the work, our girls have grown up to be workers, and as we cannot get such help elsewhere, we can only take it as another of the good gifts given to us. To have the children from the earliest days surrounded by wholesome, healthy influences, and brought up in absolute straightforwardness, surely this is something which should help towards the difficult future. If only these little ones grow up reliable and true, openings will not be difficult to find for them in the great needy field of missions. As it is, letters come asking for our girls, but we have none to spare as yet, for everything depends upon the present training, and that is why we feel we and our more earnest girls must give ourselves to it with an absorption which leaves little time for anything else.

But to come to definite details: we have two sides to the work as at present arranged. Some children become little helping nurses as soon as they are old enough, and often, such is the pressure of the work, even before. These children learn all manner of useful domestic things and become invaluable workers. Their devotion to the babies is beyond question, though there are occasional lapses, for some have difficult characters, and the best are only human after all; and trained as they are to look upon it as the most honourable as well as the happiest work, they respond by real loving service such as gladdens us many a time, and hushes our fears as to the future. The other children are being trained with the hope that some at least will become what India so much needs — evangelists, teachers, and medical missionaries. We divide the children according to the ability they show and according to their health and several bents. We do not attempt to force all into the same groove. But all of them learn the basket work which we call the Dohnavur basket work, though it is an adaptation from the North American Indian work. Miss Jacot of London has been our kind friend in this industry, and orders are now coming as quickly as they can be undertaken. The girls and older children find pleasure in this work; it fills their spare half-hours most profitably, and is their gift to the Nurseries over and above the strength of their life. For their free time is the evening hour: they work then, and can truly feel they are giving of their own.

But look at it as we may, there is only one assurance which can entirely lift off the pressure of fear for the future. It is the assurance that just as the sanctifying, directing Presence of the Lord fills our present, so by His grace it will be in the future. He will not fail us nor forsake us. Surely if He is in charge of our family, He will keep the atmosphere sweet and happy; and He will open ways by which our girls will be able to minister to the needs of this great land. Only pray for us that we may be made wise to train them to be soldiers. Soldiers not in name only, but in deed and in truth; women warriors ready to go to all lengths with their Leader, counting not their lives dear unto them. This, nothing less, is our hope and our purpose: God grant us His grace.

For always the missionary element is to the fore. The whole work is saturated with it and the twenty-fourth of the month is kept as Preaching-day, when a little band of girls goes out to the villages near Dohnavur and an equally missionary-hearted group stay at home to do the work of those who go. For nurses and teachers fit into each other, and Prayer-day and holidays usually find the school side much mixed up with the Nursery in helpful ministrations.

And so we go on, and must go on, in this attack upon the prince of darkness. We have no desire to pile up words into sensational writing, but our readers if they are to help us should understand that it is a fight, and battles are not pleasant, pretty things, and the glorious joy of battle is a very solemn joy. But, thank God, there is inspiration and courage to be had, and that without which all else fails — steadfast patience:

I have a Captain, and the heart
Of every private man
Has drunk in valour from his eyes
Since first the war began.
He is most wonderful in fight,
And of His scars a single sight
The embers of our failing might
Into a flame can fan.

I have a Guide, and in His steps
When travellers have trod,
Whether beneath was flinty rock
Or yielding grassy sod,
They cared not, but with force unspent,
Unmoved by pain they onward went,
Unstayed by pleasure still they bent
Their zealous course to God.

Only let us look long and often at the Scars, and follow hard after our Guide, and then is it not certain that He will give us power over all the power of the enemy, and direct our steps, and cause us to walk upon our high places, even those difficult future high places that we naturally fear, without stumbling. He will make room enough under us for to go.

THE END

PREENA AND HER CLASS

THE BASKET ROOM.

In a duplicate of this room the Teddies have "lessons" every day

Note

Copies of the "Dohnavur Books, and all information regarding the Fellowship, can be obtained from the Home Secretary:

Miss O. Gibson,

4, Alan Road, Wimbledon,

London, S. W. 19.

or from

The Secretary,

Dohnavur Fellowship,

Dohnavur,

Tinnevelly District,

S. India.

In Ireland, Scotland, Australia, New Zealand, Canada, South Africa, and the United States of America, friends of the work act as Hon. Secretaries and sell the books. Names and addresses of any of these will be sent on application to either of the above.

The books are also obtainable from

U. S. A. : Hope Church Sunday School Missionary Activities, Semple and Cote Brilliante Aves., St. Louis, Mo.;

Australia : The Keswick Book Depot, 315, Collins Street, Melbourne :

G. E. Heald, Esq., 18, Howard Street, Perth ;

China : The Fraternity Book Room, 216, Nathan Rd., Kowloon, Hong Kong.

Switzerland : La Maison de la Bible, 11, Rue de Rive, Geneva.

and in the ordinary way through book-sellers in any part of the world.

For hundreds of other excellent titles see:

www.**Classic***Christian***Ebooks**.com

Inspiring and uplifting classics from authors such as:

E. M. Bounds
Amy Carmichael
Alfred Edersheim
Jonathan Edwards
Charles Finney
D. L. Moody
G. Campbell Morgan
Andrew Murray
George Muller
Charles Spurgeon
Hudson Taylor
R. A. Torrey
John Wesley
…and many more!

Made in United States
Orlando, FL
12 June 2023

34042656R00046